One Little Farm

Boyhood Visits to a Midwestern Farm
in the 1920s and '30s

One Little Farm

Boyhood Visits to a Midwestern Farm
in the 1920s and '30s

written and illustrated by Donald S. Henning

Midwest Traditions, Inc.
Mount Horeb, Wisconsin
1995

Midwest Traditions, Inc. is a nonprofit educational organization devoted to the study and preservation of the folk history and traditional cultures of the American Midwest. Our publications serve to bring this diverse heritage to broader public attention.

For a catalog of books and other materials, write:
Midwest Traditions
P.O. Box 320
Mount Horeb, Wisconsin 53572 U.S.A.
(telephone 1-800-736-9189)

Library of Congress Catalog Card #95-79173

Book Design: MacLean & Tuminelly
Editor: Carol J. Henning

Publisher's Cataloging-in-Publication Data
Henning, Donald S.
    One little farm : boyhood visits to a Midwestern farm in the 1920s and '30s
/ written and illustrated by Donald S. Henning.
    p. cm.
    ISBN: 1-883953-12-X.
    1. Farm life — Middle West — History.   I. Title.
S521.H46 1995 630'.74'77
    QBI95-20407

First Edition

10 9 8 7 6 5 4 3 2 1

Dedicated to my wife,
Carol,
who has brought
so much beauty and love
to my life and
has steadfastly encouraged me
in all worthy pursuits.

Dirt Farmer

by Arden Antony

He finds beauty among these simple things;
The path a plow makes in the rich, red loam,
Gay sun-gold in ripe wheat — a plover's wings —
A cow-bell, tinkling as the herd comes home.
He treads the soil, with earth-love in his heart;
Watches the young crops spring from fertile ground,
Loves the warm rain that makes the peach buds start,
Land — and a man — in close communion bound!

from Christian Science Monitor, 1938

Table of Contents

List of Illustrations

Foreword

This book is about a farm, familiar and dear to my heart and my family's for many years. It belonged to my Uncle Frank and Aunt Carrie. Frank J. Brott, the youngest of eleven children, was born in 1883 in a log cabin on this land in Ozaukee County, Wisconsin. His father and grandfather had farmed the land before him, starting in 1825. Uncle Frank and his wife, Carrie, had no children and together worked the farm alone.

In her youth, my mother had visited the farm often and had fond memories of the place. After she was married, she and my father continued to visit (my father's sister had coincidentally married Uncle Frank's brother, so our families were doubly entwined). So I just naturally grew up enjoying our many pleasant trips to "the farm."

This book is a reconstruction, mostly from cherished memories, of what it was like in the 1920s and '30s on the farm of Frank J. Brott and his wife, Carrie, as seen through the eyes of a young city boy.

Donald S. Henning
1995

The little stone schoolhouse Uncle Frank had attended.

Introduction

This little farm in southeastern Wisconsin was typical of many places in America's Midwest. The original inhabitants were Native Americans, who moved across the land in search of wild game, fish and fowl, fruits and nuts. The first Europeans to explore the region were the French, who passed through, mostly following the waterways, on their search for military and religious glory ... and for the coveted animal furs so important to early trade.

The settlers that followed, however, were English, Irish, Scotch, Dutch, German, Swiss, and Scandinavian immigrants. Drawn by the availability of land, these hardy people began farming in the early 1800s, in some cases finding terrain, soil, and climate similar to those of their homelands. Getting started as newcomers was a severe test of their determination, courage, and endurance. Faith and luck helped.

Their first task was to fell the trees and build that basic shelter, a log cabin. Stumps had to be pulled out, rocks cleared away, and plowing done before the first crop could go in. They had to dig a shallow well, and being near a stream made raising livestock easier.

If they survived the onslaught of wind, cloudbursts, floods, lightning, drought, heat, cold, disease, and accidents, a second generation carried on the work on the same farm. Eventually, the log cabin was abandoned and the family moved into a frame house, built with lumber from a sawmill established on a river in a nearby village.

The second generation's way of life was a vast improvement over that of their parents, but still would be considered primitive by today's standards. Their food came almost entirely from their own land. Only staples like flour, coffee, tea, sugar, and salt were bought at the local mill or general store. Water for drinking and cooking came from the well, for other purposes out of a barrel or cistern where rain from the roof was channeled and stored. Their only light was from kerosene lamps. Cooking was done on a big, black cast-iron stove which, incidentally, was also a main source of heat. Absence of refrigeration necessitated preservation of food by smoke-curing, canning, pickling, or drying. Some vegetables and fruits could be kept in the root cellar. There were no closets; their meager clothing hung from hooks on the wall.

The party-line telephone, the weekly local newspaper, and the mail were their first links to the rest of the world. Then came the automobile and radio, followed in the 1930s by rural electrification.

The usual livestock consisted of Plymouth Rock, Rhode Island Red, or White Leghorn chickens, a herd of Holstein or Guernsey cattle, a pair of Percheron or Belgian draft horses and, on most farms, a few pigs, geese, ducks, or turkeys.

A symbol of thanks.

Crops were primarily corn, oats, rye, wheat, alfalfa, clover, and hay. Popular garden crops were beans, peas, cabbage, and potatoes. Barbed wire surrounded and divided most properties, with grazing cattle rotated through the fields along with the crops.

Garbage went to the pigs, dishwater to the garden or the fishing-worm bed, newspapers to the cookstove, bottles and jars to the pantry to be re-used, and other solid trash to a gravel pit in need of filling.

Today we find many of the fine old stone or brick houses still in use, some in excellent condition. Wooden houses are being restored to their original appearance and improved with modern materials. The old pumps, plows, and grindstones are carefully placed in yards as charming, decorative artifacts. Most of the old silos, corn cribs, and other outbuildings, including once-stately barns, are now crumbling, sagging, and rotting away, their wood salvaged for beamed family rooms or rustic picture frames.

The chickens and cattle haven't changed much except for the greater variety of breeds such as the Angus, the white-faced Hereford, the Jersey, the Brahma, and the Brown Swiss. Horses are still plentiful, but mostly as riding breeds kept at stables here and there. The once-common draft horses are employed mostly for show in beer commercials, circus parades, and state fair competitions.

On many a farm, cattle have been moved from spacious, verdant pastures into small, crowded feed-lots next to barns where the poor creatures stand, hoof-deep, in mud made by their own waste products. On some farms, grazing cattle have been replaced by exotic llamas, alpacas, buffalo, and emus.

To the old crops have been added beets, soybeans, and sunflowers.

The new barns are colored metal. The silos are glossy blue porcelain. The power to work the fields comes from a collection of tractors with six or eight wheels, air conditioning, and cassette decks. Many of the homes are contemporary ranch houses. Yard lights blaze from sunset to sunrise. Lightning rods on the ridgepole have been supplanted by television antennae, and where the windmill stood, there is an occasional satellite dish.

Farming has long been a tough and constant economic battle, and the farmer is entitled to all the modern buildings, vehicles, and conveniences he can manage. Still, the emotions of many of us are stirred by the sight of an old, mellow building ... by a country road bordered with tall grasses, vines, and wildflowers ... by a rustic fence neither painted nor electrified.

I hope this book will bring back warm, wonderful memories for some of you. For others who have never had the pleasure to experience life on a farm, I hope you will enjoy the education.

D. S. H.

The Brott farmyard, looking northwest.

... past barns and silos painted with huge signs ....

CHAPTER ONE

Out on a Sunday

The Brott farm was about thirty miles north of the city of Milwaukee. From the farm, it was just two miles north to the quiet little village of Waubeka. A quarter-mile east led to the Milwaukee River, threading its way south through the length of Ozaukee County, bordering Lake Michigan. It was a land of rolling hills on the eastern edge of Wisconsin.

Uncle Frank was not really my uncle, but was a sort of grand-uncle by marriage, traced back through my maternal grandmother, Nana. However, he was about the same age as my mother, who had spent a lot of time out at the Brotts' farm when she was a child. As I was growing up, visits by our family to the farm were natural and frequent occurrences as far back as I can remember.

Everyone would read aloud in unison ....

Having been born and raised in the city, I always found the farm an exciting place, in many ways a contrast to everything in my usual daily life ... the winding roads, the open land, the buildings, the animals (and the smells!). I was overjoyed any time Mother and Dad said we were going out to Brotts' farm.

Back in the 1920s the drive took about an hour in our grey Oakland with the black leatherette top. Once out of the city, the gravel roads — some oiled — were narrow, and the stone houses, windmills, grazing cattle, and wildflowers along the way added to my growing anticipation.

These excursions were, of course, more likely on pleasant days when there was no likelihood of problems with snowdrifts and muddy roads. And so, on a sunny Sunday, after church, we would have a quick lunch at home and head north on the oft-traversed, two-lane state highway, passing through one small village after another to the familiar dirt county road where we turned. We continued our journey over hills and through fertile valleys, past barns and silos painted with huge signs promoting Fisk Tires, Exide Batteries, and Wadham's Gasoline.

We waved at farmers out in their fields and they returned our greeting. Everyone would read aloud in unison an occasional series of Burma Shave signs ... "NEAR AND FAR ... HEAR 'EM HOLLER ... HALF-POUND JAR ... HALF A DOLLAR ... BURMA SHAVE!" With windows open, we encountered all the aromas, good and bad, of farming country as we rolled along.

The white farmhouse, sheltered by huge old oak and maple trees.

Hawks circled overhead. Pheasants bolted across the road or flapped wildly, taking flight. Raccoons and skunks ambled out of our way. At last we would pass the "Y" intersection with the road from Saukville, where stood the little stone schoolhouse Uncle Frank had walked to when he was a boy. When visiting as a young girl, my mother had sometimes attended school with him.

The farm was only about a mile farther, and soon we were passing the lower pasture with the spring-fed water hole where the Brotts' small herd of about a dozen Holsteins usually grazed. As we climbed the next hill, the big red barn came into view and then the white farmhouse just beyond, sheltered by huge old oak and maple trees.

My father would "beep" the horn as we coasted past to turn into the driveway and stop just behind the house.

Likely as not, the screen door would fly open, and out would come Aunt Carrie, eyes squinting in the bright sunlight, face beaming when she recognized us. She chattered a mile a minute ... how glad she was to see us and how Frank was out in the barn but he'd be right back and how were we and it had been a long time and what were we waiting for, get out and come on in the house and had we eaten ... ?

Her welcome was heartwarming, and she was as different from anyone I knew as the farm was different from the city. I was free to wander anywhere I wanted, and since there were a hundred things to see and do, I was always the first one out of the car, off to meet Uncle Frank and discover what adventures lay ahead.

The horse stalls.

CHAPTER TWO

The Lay of the Land

I can't say I remember too much about farms other than the Brotts', but it seems to me theirs was typical of many small Midwestern farms of the time. It was about forty-seven acres of rolling, fertile land, most of which was cultivated. The lower meadows were rotated for grazing, and there were a few acres of woods. About six acres at the northwest corner were occupied by the buildings, a vegetable garden, and an orchard.

Seven acres were on the other side of the county road, which runs from the town of Cedarburg, ten miles to the south, to Waubeka, two miles to the north. Neighboring farms bordered it on all sides. The land around the buildings was quite flat, with large shade trees, but just south of the barn the terrain dropped down to the farm's lowest point near the road. There, a pasture was filled with hummocks, and a spring kept a very small area wet enough for cattails and marsh marigolds.

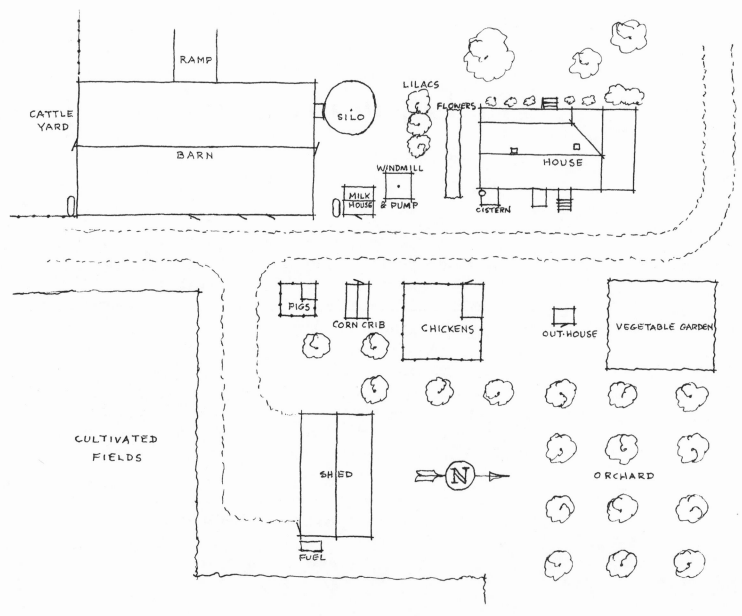

Plan of the Brott farm.

As was common in the area, the farmhouse was white, the barn red with white trim, and the smaller buildings either white or unpainted. Directly behind the house, across the gravel driveway, stood the outhouse and a good-sized vegetable garden. Beyond that grew an orchard of old apple trees of mixed varieties ... Greenings, Snow Apples, Delicious, Transparents, and a few more, the names of which I don't recall. Oh, yes ... and two cherry trees.

Just south of the outhouse was the chicken yard, with a coop big enough for chickens but cramped for humans. Next in line along the driveway, south of the chicken enclosure, came the corn crib, with a rusty old sheller. Just to the east stood the shed, housing a Model T Ford sedan, a Model T truck, some small machinery, and a big workbench. Outside stood a pedal-powered grindstone. A pig pen with a very small shelter in it completed the array of structures on the east side of the drive.

On the west side of the drive, south of the house, was a small patch of grass, a few flowers for cutting, some old lilac bushes ... then the windmill over the pump, the milk house, and the big barn, in that order. A pipe from the pump ran through the milk house to a watering trough on the other side. The stone silo was on the north end of the barn.

With its many fascinating nooks and crannies, the farmstead was a wonderful place for a youngster to explore. I always found something new to arouse my interest and keep me busy.

Bird's-eye view, looking southeast.

CHAPTER THREE

A Modest Home

Uncle Frank and Aunt Carrie had no children. Perhaps that was part of the reason they enjoyed having visitors. They lived alone in a small, two-story white house with narrow wooden siding, cedar shingles, and lightning rods. It was built in 1884, and like most houses in the neighborhood, it rested on a foundation of round fieldstones gleaned on the property. The floor plan was ell-shaped, with a front porch filling in the corner of the ell.

Since the front doors were seldom used, my description begins at the back, where a few steps led up to a small wooden porch with a simple two-by-four railing. To the left of the porch was a slanting cellar door. Near the corner of the house was a concrete slab over the cistern; on it sat the big barrel used as a filter for rainwater, delivered by two spouts from the gutters along the roof. Multi-colored hollyhocks crowded the spaces between.

The back of the house.

The drinking water pail.

Turning a white porcelain doorknob opened the paneled door to a vestibule about six feet square. A small window over the door admitted just enough light. A row of hooks behind the door held a sizeable accumulation of the more frequently used jackets, sweaters, mackinaws, scarves, and caps, which gave off a blended aroma of barn, animals, and wool. On the plank floor was an oval braided rug. Opposite the outer door was another door leading down some very steep steps to a small basement. At the foot of the stairs was a damp, dark root-cellar with bins of vegetables and apples and shelves with jars of preserves. The floor was hard-packed earth and cobwebs adorned the joists overhead. One inspection of the cellar by lantern light was quite enough for me.

Next to the cellar door was an oaken ice-box, placed there for the iceman's convenience and to keep the ice more cool in the winter than it would be in a warm kitchen.

The vestibule had a door on the right which opened into a dining room. This room was bright and cheerful, with two windows on the right facing east and one on the far northern end. Heavy ecru lace curtains were tied back halfway up. Just inside the door, to the left, was a polished, nickel-plated, pot-bellied stove with an isinglass window in the door. It rested on a large, square, tin-covered asbestos sheet which protected the painted, wide-plank floor. In the ceiling, directly over the stove, was a large iron grating, also nickel-plated, that allowed some of the rising warm air to reach the second-floor bedroom.

... just inside the door was a polished, nickel-plated, pot-bellied stove.

On a large rug in the middle of the room was an oblong oak table covered with a crocheted tablecloth. A permanent centerpiece consisted of a cut-glass bowl filled with artificial flowers. Overhead hung an ornate kerosene lamp. Four chairs sat around it, and two more in the far corners. A light oak buffet graced the left wall, with a few decorative items on it; a yellowed engraving in a simple dark frame hung above it. I recall eating in the dining room only once; that was when Uncle Frank's brother, Henry, died, and there was a small family gathering. The rest of the meals were eaten in the kitchen.

Between the stove and the buffet was a large doorway with two doors that rolled into the walls, leading to the next room, the parlor. That room, like the dining room, was opened only for special occasions such as a funeral or a visit by relatives from distant cities or overseas, and had a slightly musty odor. It, too, had two windows in the long wall opposite the door and one in the end wall to the right.

On the left parlor wall was a door, rarely used, to the front porch. A small, brown mohair davenport or settee rested between the windows, embellished with a couple of suede pillows bearing burned designs such as "Home Sweet Home" or "Chicago."

On the inside wall opposite was a heavy, oblong table partly covered with a green velvet runner with gold silk fringe and

In the dining room.

tassels, and on it sat a wind-up Edison cylinder phonograph with a morning-glory horn. Underneath, on an open shelf, was a good supply of boxed cylinders with labels identifying Sousa marches, operatic solos, and a few tear-jerkers from before World War I. In the far corner, diagonally across from the door, stood a huge, yellowish secretary of bird's-eye maple ... one of those asymmetric combinations of fold-down desk and glass-front display cabinet, filled with small mementos from everywhere. The large ingrain rug, heavy window drapes, three or four chairs, two kerosene lamps, and some fancy gold-framed prints of paintings popular at the time completed the room.

From the back vestibule, a door to the left led into the kitchen — a room discussed in more detail later — with its adjacent pantry and bedroom. Ninety-eight percent of life in the house was spent in those three rooms.

Upstairs were a sparsely-furnished bedroom and an attic storage space, accessible by a stairway off the kitchen.

That was it ... small, plain, no running water, no indoor water-closet or bathtub, and for most of its years, no electricity. Furniture stayed for generations and was never rearranged. Like that of many farmers around them, the home of Uncle Frank and Aunt Carrie was a simple, modest shelter, a center for a life that was often hard and demanding.

The wind-up phonograph.

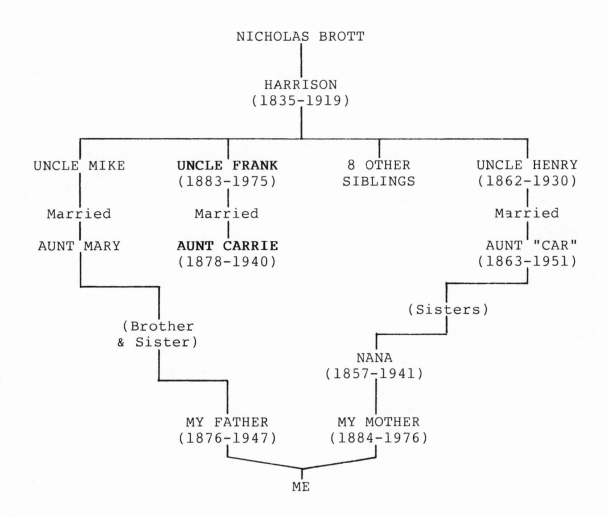

NICHOLAS BROTT

HARRISON
(1835-1919)

UNCLE MIKE

UNCLE FRANK
(1883-1975)

8 OTHER
SIBLINGS

UNCLE HENRY
(1862-1930)

Married

Married

Married

AUNT MARY

AUNT CARRIE
(1878-1940)

AUNT "CAR"
(1863-1951)

(Brother
& Sister)

(Sisters)

NANA
(1857-1941)

MY FATHER
(1876-1947)

MY MOTHER
(1884-1976)

ME

The family circle.

CHAPTER FOUR

Uncle Frank

Nicholas Brott was the first of his family to farm the land, settling there about 1825. His son, Harrison, sired eleven children. Frank Brott was one of them, born in 1883. One of his older brothers married a sister of my grandmother's, which made Frank a kind of uncle to my mother. However, Uncle Frank and my mother were only a year apart in age, and they had spent many happy days together on the farm when she visited as a girl. During the span of years when I saw him, Uncle Frank was in his forties and fifties. He always impressed me as being a big man, though it may have been due to my being a rather skinny kid in my early years.

He was a little shy of six feet tall and had the muscular build of a man who had spent much of his life guiding a horse-drawn plow and other implements through the rocky but fertile soil found in the area. His large chest was matched by his stomach, which showed the results of catering to the appetite of an outdoor man, and though he was busy from sunrise to sunset, he managed to carry enough weight to be called portly.

Uncle Frank.

He had an angular face, with high cheekbones and a somewhat aquiline nose, long and thin. This, augmented by his short, straight, black hair (edged with a little grey) and his weathered, tan skin, gave him an almost Indian-like appearance. His brother, Mike, who lived in Seattle and, by coincidence, was married to my father's sister, Mary, had a similar appearance, especially the cheekbones.

Bib-type, blue denim overalls and a matching jacket were his usual costume, and under them, an old white or blue shirt, always buttoned at the neck. At any time of year, the long underwear showed at the wrists. Heavy, high work shoes were always worn except to church.

Uncle Frank had a nasal twang to his voice and a loud hearty laugh that surfaced easily. With a twinkle in his eye, he had a wonderful sense of humor. If he happened to be near the house as we drove into the yard, he might keep a very sober face and say, "By God, too bad we didn't know you were comin'. We're just gonna get ready to leave; gotta go in to Port Washington today." As my parents registered utter disappointment, he'd look at me and wink and then say, "Oh well, guess we'll have to hang around a while to be polite!" Then he'd burst out laughing and say, "Come on in! How are yuh, anyway?"

The church in the nearby village.

I couldn't help but admire this man who knew so much about so many things foreign to me, and who single-handed was able to accomplish so much with his horses and rattling, rusty equipment. I could feel his strength as we'd walk along with his big hand on my shoulder, his heavy denim rustling with each step. He had a slow, deliberate gait, as if he were always stepping in the loose, uneven soil of a plowed field. A slight limp remained from a leg badly broken years ago when one of his big draft horses got out of hand in the stall.

He was the treasurer of the church in the village two miles north. Every Sunday, with few exceptions, he dressed up in his dark blue suit, accompanied by a slightly jaundiced white shirt with a curled-up collar, yellow tie, and high brown shoes. Alone or with his wife, he drove the Model T in to church.

Bad times or good, the chores had to be done, and Uncle Frank seemed to have willingly accepted the life that took such devotion and gave many disappointments. Complaints were few and visits with him were always happy ones.

A good man, Uncle Frank.

... the room was dominated by the huge, black cast-iron range.

CHAPTER FIVE

In the Kitchen

As with so many early farmhouses, Frank and Carrie Brott's kitchen was the scene of most of the daily activity. Here was the preparation and eating of meals, major and minor bathing, the only indoor water supply, the setting for neighbors' visits, occasional telephone calls, washing, ironing, mending, reading, writing, and resting. Today it would be called a "living center."

The woodwork, like that throughout the house, was light-brown painted "wood-grain." Well-worn linoleum covered the floor, and oval braided rugs lay at the sink and front door. The uneven plastered walls and ceiling were painted white above the wainscoting.

Instead of a skinny-legged gas stove like that in our kitchen at home, the room was dominated by the huge, black cast-iron range. It squatted on an asbestos pad covered with painted tin, hugging the floor, and seemed to have no end of doors and lids and handles. From a big pine woodbox on its left, various sized twigs and split branches were shoved into the small left front door, and the slots in the door were adjusted to keep the fire just right ... blazing while the food was being cooked, glowing gently at other times to keep the room warm or the water hot. Hanging over on the right end was the hot water tank, filled from the pump and ladled out as needed.

The bottom contained a huge oven with a thermometer built into the door, and the top had four places for heating up pots, kettles, and skillets. The teakettle and coffee pot usually occupied the back lids. Partway up the stove pipe, at the back, was the warming oven.

Altogether, it was a fascinating, clever monster from which came all manner of good things. Behind it, leaning against the chimney, were Uncle Frank's rifle and shotgun, and on the floor, a can of stove blacking with which Aunt Carrie lovingly kept her pride-and-joy looking like new.

In the front corner of the room, to the right of the stove, was a door to a very small bedroom, its location, no doubt, planned to take advantage of some heat from the stove. On the front wall were a window, a door to the porch, and the fascinating oak wall-telephone, with its receiver hanging on the left, a crank on the right, two bells on the top, a long swivel mouthpiece in front, an inclined surface for a pad of paper ... and neighbors listening in on every call. I can still see diminutive Aunt Carrie standing on tiptoes, with her neck craned, shouting toward the mouthpiece.

The wall opposite the stove had a door leading to a steep stairway to the second floor. Next to it on the right rested a lumpy, squeaky chaise with golden-colored mohair upholstery. Above

The wall telephone.

it hung a black-framed, faded old print of an English garden. In the far right corner, a door opened into the back hall.

The remaining east wall had a window, a big calendar, and an oaken clock whose pendulum tick-tocked very loudly. Under it was a big rocking chair. In the right corner was a wooden cabinet, with a well-scrubbed maple top, a chipped white porcelain sink, and a noisy little red hand-pump to bring up water from the cistern for dishes and bathing. A flaked mirror hung on the wall back of the sink, and to the right of the pump, on a ridged roller, hung a striped cotton towel.

Next to the sink, on the same wall as the stove, was the door to the pantry ... a wonderful, bright little room! Below the counters, cabinet doors concealed bags of flour, sugar, and salt. The shelves above, on three walls, were all covered with white oilcloth. Here were stacks of shiny dishes, cups, and bowls ... some plain white, some fancy and rimmed with gold. Rows of heavy tumblers stood next to a few pieces of cut-glass stemware. Cans, jars, and tin boxes were everywhere ... tea, coffee, sugar, flour, salt, vinegar, jars of fruit, pickles, vegetables, and jam. A divided tray held the everyday eating utensils. On the right, just inside the door, was a big, white porcelain enameled pail with a matching cover, from which extended the handle of a matching dipper. This was the source of water reserved for drinking and cooking, clear and so good, carried in from the well-pump some distance from the house.

... with its well-scrubbed maple top, white porcelain sink, and red hand-pump.

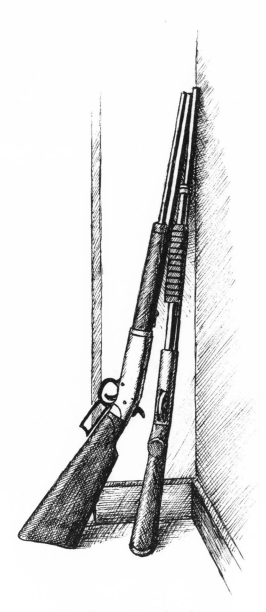

Leaning against the chimney.

In the center of the kitchen stood a big, round, oak pedestal table, usually covered with a flowered oilcloth, and four pressed-back chairs. Over it hung a simple kerosene lamp with a big glass shade. Grouped in the center were the salt and pepper shakers, a sugar bowl, reading glasses, the latest newspaper, and a small collection of recent mail.

When there was cooking to be done, the big table was where all the preparations were made ... the flour sifting, the mixing, the potato peeling, pea shelling, apple paring and slicing, berry cleaning, cherry pitting, dough kneading (for bread) and rolling (for pies and cookies), and filling of jars with fruits, pickled vegetables, jams, jellies, ketchup, and relishes.

In the pantry ... a wonderful bright little room!

There were few books in the kitchen. On a wall shelf were a couple of children's books for me or my three cousins — Frank, Ken, and Harry Collis — who occasionally visited at the same time I did. There were catalogs from Sears, Roebuck & Co. and Montgomery Ward, a small local telephone directory, the Bible, a hymnal, a prayer book, a ragged notebook of scribbled recipes, and a well-worn photo album. From spring to fall, there was little time for reading, other than the weekly newspaper issued from the county seat, Port Washington.

Their kitchen truly was the heart of the home. Its walls wrapped protectively around all who entered into this center of a simple, self-sufficient life.

On the kitchen table.

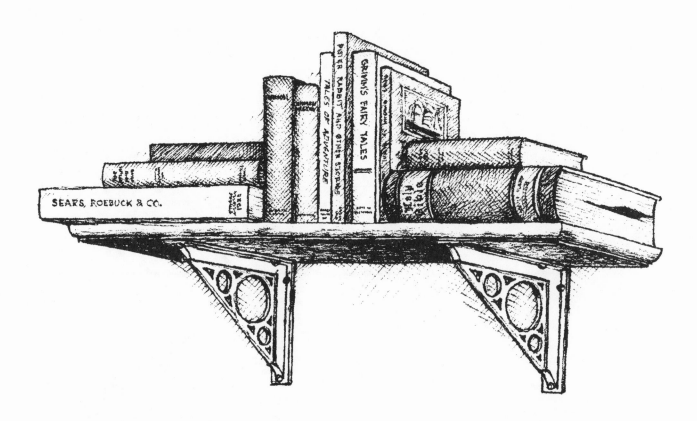

The wall shelf of books.

CHAPTER SIX

Aunt Carrie

Her real name was Carrie, but when she wasn't present, those who loved her called her "Tin Lizzie." I wish I had an explanation for that nickname, but my last chance died when my mother did. It was said fondly, for she had a heart of gold, a wonderful sense of humor, and a penchant for hard work. Her generosity and kindness made her instantly lovable to children. She could be referred to, however, as a "character."

She was short … hardly five feet … and wiry, with nothing but muscle and skin thinly covering her bones. Her greying brown hair was pulled tightly and arranged in a knot at the top. I don't think she ever owned any makeup.

Neither did she own an extensive wardrobe. It was, in fact, meager … a few simple, rather long, drab-colored cotton dresses, a fancy one for Sundays, and always the same black high-button shoes.

Aunt Carrie.

She had good teeth — real or false — and her ready, broad smile showed them off as a matter of course. Her eyes had a twinkle and when she smiled they practically closed. The crow's-feet wrinkles must have been as much from laughter as from the bright sun.

She had two voices, as different as day and night. Talking loudly, she had a rather raucous, hen-like squawk that reached into a falsetto range when she got excited or laughed. Just as quickly, she would get serious and speak with a soft, humming contralto. Most of the time her high-pitched, rapid chatter sounded like a thirty-three r.p.m. record … played at seventy-eight.

Behind it was genuine enthusiasm. Her own cares were brushed aside to listen to others and what had been happening in their lives. A staunch church-goer, she could never have had an unkind thought about anyone. Hers was a hard life, sharing the chores with Uncle Frank from sun-up to bedtime, with no children or hired hands to share the load. Mishaps were taken in stride … she'd had her share of bruises and broken bones, and once suffered burns on her face and arms when a frying pan's contents burst into flames.

No one could have made a guest feel more welcome. She truly enjoyed it when my cousin, Ken, and myself were there, either separately or together. Any activity had her blessing as long as it wasn't dangerous, and treats from her cookie jar were frequent.

There had better be enough room in the car when "Tin Lizzie" bade you good-bye, because produce and preserves were loaded in until the doors wouldn't close. On the way home we might have to share the back seat with one or two dozen apples, two heads of cabbage, a big bunch of carrots, a dozen ears of corn, a few beets, some radishes, six or eight tomatoes, two green peppers, a dozen eggs, and several jars of preserves.

Though she was only sixty-two when she died, she always seemed older. Perhaps, being small, she had suffered a greater strain from the rigorous farming life. I was away at college the last years of her life, but I shall always remember Aunt Carrie's smile, her laughing eyes, her voice, and her gentleness.

Truly, good things did come in a small package.

Fruits of the harvest.

CHAPTER SEVEN

The Barn

Bank barns, so-called because they originally were built into the side of an embankment or hill, are the most prevalent type in the farmlands of the Midwest. The lower level, with walls of fieldstone, concrete block, or poured concrete, is fully exposed on one side and both ends. On the opposite side, an earthen ramp leads to the upper level with its threshing floor, grain bins, and hay mows.

Brotts' was that type, a five-bay barn about eighty feet long and forty feet wide. Sawn cedar shingles covered the gable roof, with a half-dozen lightning rods along the ridge. The upper sides were plain, vertical pine boards. The lower level walls, two feet thick, were built of fieldstone, with heavy oak timbers over the doors and windows. During the years of my visits, the barn was painted red, with white on the trim and stone walls.

The stone silo, with shingled roof.

Its orientation offered protection from the north winds. The big door at the top of the ramp faced west, and on the lower level, the door to the milking area opened to the south.

I remember vividly my first visit to the threshing floor. The barn rafters and ceiling seemed so big and high I couldn't imagine how the builders got up there to put it all in place. It was very dark at first, but as my eyes got accustomed to it I could make out the overhead track, ropes, and hay-fork used to unload a wagon and drop the hay in a huge pile in the mow. The wooden sides, which looked so snugly fitted from the outside, now showed hundreds of narrow gaps between the boards ... on a dry day. In wet weather, they and all the little pinpoints of light in the roof would disappear as the boards and shingles swelled up.

High up on each end, some light came in through diagonally placed windows, diffused by an accumulation of decades of dust. Sparrows chirped somewhere in the dark, and barn swallows swooped and zoomed to their nests high up in the purlins.

In the lower level, the stable for the horses and cows always smelled with strong odors of urine and manure. In contrast, up there on the second level the air was dry and sweet-smelling. Depending on the season, the center floor might have the haywagon on it. Beyond the mowsteads — the low wooden walls bordering the center floor — the huge store of alfalfa or clover for winter feeding was kept on one end of the barn, and straw for year-round bedding was stored on the other.

Up on the threshing floor, the air was dry and sweet-smelling.

A hay fork.

A ladder with time-worn, polished rungs on one of the posts provided means for climbing up to the top of the straw in the mow and sliding or jumping off to a comfortable pile on the floor. This was my favorite place to play. When any of my cousins — Ken, Frank, or Harry — were out there we could spend hours in the barn.

On the far side of the floor, under a trap door, was a steep stairway to the lower level. Through it were thrown forkfuls of straw for bedding the cows and horses, and hay for feeding them.

Opposite the stairway was the granary. Dusty windows shed dim light into the small room where bins of corn, oats, and wheat were filled to overflowing. It was a wonderful sensation to dig one's hand and arm deep down into the grain and feel the touch of millions of kernels caressing the skin.

Down below, a wide Dutch door in the middle of the south end opened to the milking room, which occupied almost half the lower level. There were a half-dozen small windows set in the thick walls, with a collection of old cans, bottles, and other things sitting on the recessed sills. Big blue flies buzzed around and banged into the windows. A four-foot aisle along each of the side walls allowed Uncle Frank room to put feed for the cows in the troughs under the stanchions. When the cows were in place, this left an aisle about eight feet wide in the middle of the room. The west aisle also had overhead chutes, for obtaining grain from the granary bins on the floor above.

Dusty windows shed dim light into the small granary ....

A low wooden wall and door separated this area from the north end of the barn. On the other side were pens for the calves and heifers. A Dutch door on the north end allowed entry there as well. Outside, on the north half of the east side were a series of Dutch doors to the horse stalls where Uncle Frank kept his two huge Percherons. As a child, I thought them so gigantic they seemed like creatures from another world. To me, they seemed far bigger than most horses seen commonly in the streets and alleys of Milwaukee pulling wagons of milk, bakery, vegetables, and junk. I remember Uncle Frank's loud, sharp commands as he held the bridle of one of his Percherons and backed it into its stall. They were powerful beasts, and could very easily cause accidental injury. Uncle Frank walked with a slight limp since one such occasion.

The stone silo, with a shingled roof, stood near one corner of the barn, connected by a short stone-and-concrete passage with a wooden door. This was the only major thing about the farm that always remained a mystery to me. The heady aroma emanating from the door I would later learn was the sweet smell of fermented cornstalks ... rich nutritional silage for the cattle.

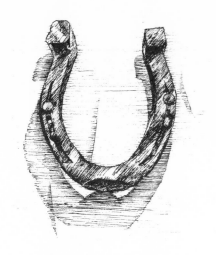

Properly hung so good luck doesn't "run out."

A barn is the most costly and vital building on a farm, as many an unlucky farmer has discovered when tightly-packed, damp hay got hot enough to spontaneously ignite. Help came from everywhere when a barn caught fire, but everyone knew the best to be hoped for was rescuing the livestock. One of life's saddest, most devastating sights is the smoldering, flattened ruins of a barn the day after, with the confused cattle standing nearby.

Uncle Frank always took special care when he had to use a kerosene lantern at milking time. The mixed fragrance of evenings in the barn ... fresh milk and lantern fumes and the gifts the cows deposited on the floor ... was a sensation I well remember, but one I'm content to live without.

A hay hook for grabbing bales.

CHAPTER EIGHT

Milking Time

On one visit to the farm, when I was about eight years old, Uncle Frank said, "Come on, Donald ... let's go milk the cows!"

We walked along the gravel drive, stopping first at the milk house, where he set clean, shiny milk cans and a pail on a cart and pushed it to the far end of the barn. As we rounded the corner, I saw the herd of ten or twelve black-and-white Holsteins watching us expectantly from the barnyard gate, having already come up from the lower pasture by themselves.

That cows actually knew the right time to stop grazing and walk back to the barn was just the first thing that surprised me that day!

The herd of Holsteins watched us expectantly.

When Uncle Frank lifted a wire loop and swung the creaking wooden gate open, they slowly crossed the barnyard in single file, very lady-like, and entered the barn. That was another surprise. But when they got inside ... that did it! Each of those cows sauntered very deliberately to one particular spot that was hers — not necessarily the first empty space — and promptly put her head into the stanchion. They stood in the same order every time! Uncle Frank went around and walked down the line, pushing the stanchions shut in quick succession.

Then he disappeared up the stairway in the corner. Big clumps of alfalfa began tumbling down the stairs from the opening at the top. When a huge heap had accumulated, he came back down. With his hay fork, he distributed the fodder in the trough along the floor, under a row of bovine faces intently watching us. They began picking it up with their mouths, chomping away with a constant shushing sound, while Uncle Frank added scoops of silage from a wheelbarrow.

He went out and returned in a moment with the milk cart and parked it just inside the door. Taking the pail from the cart and a wooden stool from the corner, he went to the first cow, calling her by name. "Get over there, Belle!" He gently nudged her to the left and sat down on the stool, placing the pail between his knees.

A team of mousers.

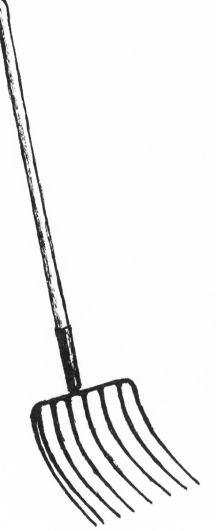

A manure fork.

There was no washing teats with antiseptic solutions in those days, and no attaching milking machines. Uncle Frank gave each teat a couple gentle pulls to remove any loose dirt, and soon I heard the rhythmic "ssshi-ssshu-ssshi-ssshu" of the milk squirting into the pail. Metallic at first, the sound became softer and deeper as the rich milk began to build up a head of foam. The filled pail was then carried over and poured into a milk can.

By then three or four barn-cats of various colors had materialized. Uncle Frank poured some milk in an old pie pan for them — small payment for these hard-working mousers. Then he poured more into a dipper and gave it to me. Unfortunately (but for their own protection), very few people today know the pleasure of warm, creamy, fresh milk.

He moved down the line steadily, as the late sunlight filtered through the windows. I followed him every step as he continued filling pail after pail until the last drop was taken from the last donor. He knew them all by name … Belle, Sarah, Kate, Daisy. A couple of the names, I noticed, coincided with those of his relatives or neighbors. The cart, with its load of filled cans, was wheeled out to the milk house. There the cans were lifted into a big open tank of cold water, freshly pumped by the windmill just outside — or on calm, windless days, by a one-cylinder gasoline engine—and conveyed inside by a pipe through the wall.

The cans were lifted into a big open tank of cold water.

Milking done, Uncle Frank opened the stanchions and the herd slowly ambled back outside. He quickly handled the task of cleaning up the floor and spreading a little fresh straw in each place.

A little later, the milk truck, with its noisy chain drive, chugged up to the milk house. The cans were lifted up and set in the back, while clean empty ones were left to be filled the next morning.

I realized in later years what devotion to duty is required of a dairy farmer. Time and tide wait for no man, but milk cows do … twice a day, every day.

The milk cart.

The outside was vertical board-and-batten, topped with a shingled shed roof.

CHAPTER NINE

Room With a View

My earliest recollections of sanitary plumbing go back to the oak wooden tank high on the wall in our home in Milwaukee, operated by a chain and matching oak handle, that produced a loud "ker-ploonge" when pulled. That struck me as very modern when contrasted with the silent simplicity of an outhouse.

Brotts' outhouse was a "three-holer" (large, medium, and small) located just a short, leisurely stroll (or a fast run) from the back door, depending on the weather or one's sense of urgency.

It faced east, away from the house and road, toward the fields and the orchard. About three feet by five feet, the outside was vertical board-and-batten, topped with a shingled shed roof. There was a very small window in each side. A diamond-shaped cut-out in the door, covered with screening, admitted light and air ... in winter too much air, in summer not enough. Hardware consisted of rusty hinges, handles, and hooks-and-eyes to keep the door shut.

I could leave the door open and enjoy the view.

Time has been kind in letting me forget the few trips I made to this unheated retreat in the cold, snow, and wind of winter, but I vividly recall the pleasures of its use on sunny summer days. Having ascertained where everyone else was, I could leave the door open and enjoy the view of the fields, the orchard, the distant woods, the sky and drifting clouds. I could share a brief spell with the birds, butterflies, and wildflowers, and other visitors ... bees! The latter I learned to ignore, though their presence gave me a chill even on the hottest days.

The decor was aged knotty-pine walls with matching floor, ceiling, and seat. That long seat, with three individual hinged covers, I always felt needed a lot of patient, loving contouring, blending and smoothing with sandpaper. In winter, I suppose, it didn't matter much ... fast in, fast out ... but in summer, when one would prefer to linger, it left a deep impression and kept one moving around to prevent permanent scarring. It was not conducive to a relaxed appreciation of the idyllic setting.

There were accessories to occupy one's time when the weather required the door to be closed. Since I never saw a Sears, Roebuck & Co. catalog anywhere else in those early years, that served for a lot of research. It was educational to me on women's intimate apparel, medical appliances, farm machinery, tools, toys, guns ... a true book of revelation. Then there was the calendar art collection, with pictures of shy little girls in sunbonnets, landscapes in faded primary colors, and robust, healthy-looking farm animals. The star attraction was the top of a calendar from the Cunard Steamship Lines, probably sent to them because Aunt Carrie had come from

England on one of their ships. It had little glass sparkles all over its fancy, embossed surface, which framed a faded-colored picture of a beautiful big steamship with three smokestacks. Below the picture was a projecting pocket of the same material, presumably to hold treasured postcards or letters.

Yes, the necessity was there, too ... several rolls of it, and a fly swatter hung in the corner. It was made of wire screening, edged with brightly colored yarn and featuring a big red yarn rose.

Our family wasn't one to share the intimacies of the bathroom, so, after my first parental orientation when I was quite small, my flights to the outhouse were strictly solo. Whether those visits were as an observer of nature, a reader, a gallery gazer, or just a thinker depended on the weather, the time of day, and how new the Sears catalog was.

The fly swatter.

CHAPTER TEN

Fishing

As mentioned earlier, the Brotts' land was only a quarter-mile from the big Milwaukee River, winding its way to Lake Michigan thirty miles downstream. In those days of my childhood it ran clear enough for swimming and fishing, and if you accidentally got a mouthful, no harm was done.

Except for a day or so following a heavy rain, the Milwaukee is a slow-flowing river in Ozaukee County, wide and not too deep ... maybe three or four feet at the most. It was an ideal habitat for pan fish, but these were seldom on the menu at the farm. There were a couple of bamboo poles out in the shed, but Uncle Frank and Aunt Carrie never felt they could spare the time to fish. They did encourage visitors to do it, though, and had one corner of the garden, where worms thrived in loam, occasionally treated with dishwater or coffee grounds. A little effort with a spade was enough to fill a can.

With eyes transfixed on the corks, we'd wait.

On one or two visits, my mother and father and I walked along the fence lines of the cultivated fields to the farthest meadow of the farm. We were escorted by noisy crows, scurrying gophers, gliding butterflies, and busy bees. Crossing the meadow, we went up and down the small hills, through the woods to the river bank. There, in complete privacy and serenity, we would lounge in the sweet-smelling, sun-drenched grasses and wildflowers and try our luck. Turtles, their leisurely sunning interrupted, would promptly slip from a rock into the water. A kingfisher sat on a tree branch over-hanging the river, quietly biding his time until a minnow surfaced, then dove down and zoomed up with his catch. Iridescent dragonflies hovered and darted spasmodically.

I soon learned how to hold the slippery, wriggling worms and put them on the hook. With the cork bobber adjusted for the right depth, we would swing the poles out and plop the lines into the quiet, drifting water. Then, with eyes transfixed on the corks, we'd wait, interpreting any little movement as the nibble prior to complete submergence.

With the impatience of most children, I would raise my pole and recast the line over and over. Then someone would cry, "I've got one!" We'd stare at the arched pole; the taut, maneuvering line told us, indeed, a fish was hooked.

The good luck was confirmed as the pole was raised high and the line swung to shore with a wildly flipping, shiny load. A beautiful perch or sunfish dropped on the grass. I learned the hard way how to carefully approach the captive along the line and around the head, to avoid a painful puncture from its fins, remove the hook, and put the fish on a stringer.

I also found that catching two fish within a couple of minutes was no indication of a pattern, because it might easily be a quarter-hour wait for the next nibble. But after an hour or so we'd be ready to walk back with enough fish for a meal ... after cleaning the fish, of course, and cleaning up the mess, and then cleaning up me.

Soon the catch, having been dipped in egg and flour, salt and pepper, was sizzling in Aunt Carrie's big cast-iron skillet, to be served for supper along with crisp brown fried potatoes and coleslaw.

As the youngest one at the table, I felt proud to have contributed my fair share to that delicious evening meal.

Enough for a meal.

CHAPTER ELEVEN

The Shed and the Corn Crib

The future engineer dormant in me was fascinated by Uncle Frank's equipment shed. It was a wide, gable-roofed building, with three pairs of big doors, behind which were all sorts of wonderful things.

The most obvious, of course, were his two Model T Fords. One was a shiny black sedan, and the other, their not-so-shiny black pick-up truck. I had occasion to ride in both ... the former when I went along to church one Sunday, the latter when Uncle Frank had to get supplies at the mill in town.

Incidentally, the trips to the mill were exciting in their own way. The truck was loaded up with burlap bags of kernel corn. At the mill they were weighed and exchanged for bags of corn that had already been cracked, with cash changing hands for the difference in value. I liked the inside of the mill with its gears and shafts and chutes for grinding and bagging. Outside was the Milwaukee River, spilling over the dam, turning the big wheel that operated the machinery.

Getting supplies at the mill.

As my father had traded our own Model T for an Oakland when I was only six years old, I had not been old enough to learn much about it. With its high, black, skinny tires, with its odd levers at the steering wheel and three diamond-shaped foot-pedals, the vehicle became more intriguing with each passing year as my mechanical aptitude grew. I was not yet mature enough to be concerned with what was under the hood. But I did love to look at the driving controls, sitting at the wheel, and pretend I was maneuvering my way along endless roads through strange lands.

The shed had windows on either end. Through the one facing east the sunlight, dimmed by years of dust and spider webs, softly bathed a big workbench. It was almost completely covered by an accumulation of nuts, bolts, nails, parts, tools, shavings, and sawdust. Under it and on either side the collection extended, with larger parts and various sized pieces of wood and metal. Hanging on the wall and from the rafters were all manner of implements, tires, wheels, ropes, chains, and leather harnesses for the horses.

Birds flew to and from nests up under the roof. Field mice scurried along the floor. Inquisitive chickens pecked their way in and out again. Big horseflies buzzed and bumped around the windows, and bees came and went.

Sunlight, dimmed by years of dust and spider webs, softly bathed a big workbench.

As I became accustomed to the subdued light, I saw a variety of strange, rusty pieces of farm equipment. Some seemed to have been stored for a short while. The dust on others indicated they had been sitting there unused, perhaps for decades.

I loved to poke around and try to figure out what all these things were for and touch them. I liked the smell of the shed ... a mellow blend of oil and leather and wood and earth.

Just outside was a grindstone, big, round and white, in its rusty metal frame, with a seat and one pedal. Over the wheel, suspended from a bent wire, was a tin can with a small hole in the bottom. Filled at the pump, it dripped slowly onto the wheel while I pedaled away and tried my hand at sharpening a knife or an axe.

A few steps away, between the shed and the corn crib, was a still more intriguing device ... a corn sheller. A crank on the side of this cast-iron machine turned a heavy disc on the inside that was covered with hundreds of small bumps. A dried ear of corn, inserted in the funnel-like hole at the top, was squeezed and rotated between the disc and the housing. With a rattling noise, the grains of corn spewed out the bottom, and the skinny, stripped cob finally fell out, too. That was one chore I looked forward to.

A corn sheller.

The corn crib, with its tapered sides and open slat construction, was especially enjoyed when my cousin, Ken, and I were out there together. After the corn had dried on the stalks, they were husked and the crib was crammed full of the golden ears right up to the roof. By summer enough had been taken away in the wheelbarrow to feed the pigs and the chickens so we could go inside. Then the crib became a castle or a jail or a ship. This structure fell prey to a disease common to corn cribs ... it began to lean from the north wind and kept trying to fall over. The more it tried, the more Uncle Frank prevented it by propping a stick or pole against it, until eventually it had nine such crutches!

When I was quite young I had the urge to take a photo of the crib with its nine props; that photo is the frontispiece for this book. I must have recognized the artistic quality of this colorful little lopsided building, and the picture is a treasured reminder of those happy days.

A grindstone.

CHAPTER TWELVE

The Chicken Coop and the Pig Pen

It was always great fun being allowed to gather eggs. Having seen them at the grocer's had given me no clue to where those simple white objects came from, by what process they were made, or how they got to the store.

Uncle Frank and Aunt Carrie had a flock of about thirty White Leghorn hens and a rooster. They were kept in a pen about fifteen by twenty feet, with a white shed-roofed chicken coop at one corner, accessible to humans at one end by a small door. On the south side, a little square opening with a ramp outside provided escape for the chickens, who took advantage of it the instant the door was opened. Their quick departure was accompanied by clouds of dust, flying feathers, and the deafening, discordant squawking of panicked hens as they jammed the exit.

In the chicken coop.

When the dust had settled, by the dim light entering through glass windows that had never been washed, I made my search of the nesting boxes on the wall opposite the windows. Scattered here and there in the nests were shiny, white glass eggs, used for reminding the hens what they were supposed to do and where. I went from box to box, lifting out the smooth, warm, fresh eggs and gently laying them in Aunt Carrie's basket.

There were several holes in the fence large enough for the hens to squeeze through. So, after emerging from the chicken coop, I searched the grounds around the pen and nearby equipment shed for eggs, frequently finding another half-dozen or so in secluded places.

When I proudly took my precious load into the house, Aunt Carrie, in the most charitable way possible, although with amusement, pointed out that in my innocence (and ignorance) I had mixed the eggs. The fresh ones laid in the hen house couldn't be told from those so casually deposited around the yard, which were of questionable age!

Oh, well. It was fun anyway ... sort of like emerging victorious from a game played at many picnics years ago: digging for pennies in a sawdust pile. I was especially thrilled when I found one egg that was much longer than the rest. With a smile, Aunt Carrie told me it was a real find ... a rooster egg!

The pig pen was rather commonplace. It was a rail-fenced enclosure about ten feet square, with a crude shelter in one corner. In another corner rested a trough of mixed corn and garbage. Depending on the weather, dry dirt or mud was everywhere else.

I couldn't work up much interest in the huge sow who squinted and grunted at me, but it was fun to watch her litter of wiggling, squealing piglets when they were very small.

Perhaps I was more interested in the cows and chickens because their end products of milk and eggs, seen in our kitchen at home, were so easily identified right there on the farm. Maybe, too, as I ate my breakfast of ham and eggs, my naive young mind preferred not to think about the future of the pig.

Laid by a truant hen.

CHAPTER THIRTEEN

Overnight Stay

Sometimes my mother and I stayed overnight at the farm when I was quite small. I was impressed with how different life was for farmfolk with no central heat, no radio, no indoor plumbing and, in the earlier years, no electricity.

After the dinner dishes were washed, dried, and returned to the pantry, the kerosene lamps were lit. Mother and Aunt Carrie would sit at the big round table, to talk and sew, or play cards, or look at photo albums or recipes or whatever else they had saved to share.

Uncle Frank would return from taking care of the cattle and horses for the night. He settled in the rocking chair to read the local paper, joining in the conversation now and then. There was a lot of talk about times past and people I didn't know.

... with curved arms supporting a beveled mirror.

I would start the evening at the table, usually drawing pictures with a pencil in my Vireo or Big 5 tablet. In the dim light, it was easy for the day's fresh air and expenditure of energy to catch up with me, and I would soon lie down on the velour lounge. My squirming around to get comfortable was accompanied by the squeaking of its loose joints and the rustle of the lumpy excelsior with which it was stuffed. I'd page through some book or magazine until drowsiness overtook me and I'd fall asleep to the distant, fading sound of voices, the words running together, dreamlike, in a lulling murmur.

At home, this early hour would have found me wide awake, with no thought of going to bed, but out at the farm the warmth and coziness of the kitchen made me slip away quite willingly.

Sometimes I was jolted awake by the strange, uneven ringing of the old wall telephone. If the pattern of rings was proper, Aunt Carrie or Uncle Frank would get up and answer it. For Aunt Carrie this meant standing on tiptoe, craning her neck and speaking very loudly as she looked up toward the mouthpiece, holding the long receiver to her ear.

When it was time to go to bed, I was gently awakened and led by flickering lantern light up the steep, dark, painted stairs to the second floor. Making a left turn at the top, we opened the door and walked into the upper bedroom, crossing the iron grating located directly over the woodburning stove in the dining room below. In winter, warm air would be gently rising through it; it was the only source of heat up there.

The bedroom was basic and sparsely furnished, with walls painted white and wide plank floor painted brown. The windows had plain sheer ecru curtains and tan shades. A thin, worn ingrain rug covered a large part of the floor. The dominant item was the big wooden bed with a feather-filled comforter and a faded quilt. The few other furnishings were a clothes rack on the wall, two painted pressed-wood chairs, a big maple dresser, and a yellow oak commode with curved arms supporting a beveled mirror. On it were a few turkish towels and wash cloths, a dish holding a bar of soap, and a huge white china bowl with an equally big pitcher of water.

There was one other item. It was kept under the bed. Apparently it caused everyone embarrassment, because they would always refer to it as a "thundermug." To children it was a "potty." Technically, I believe it was called a chamber pot. In any case, I only used it once or twice when I was very small and couldn't avoid it. To this day I carry chilling memories of my bottom touching that cold china! It was awkward enough so that I soon planned my fluid consumption and trips to the outhouse to avoid needing to use it.

The feather bed made up for a lot of things in this simple life of few amenities, especially on a blustery winter night. It was like suddenly being transported to a tropical cloud. Such warmth and softness and feeling of snug isolation from the world has no equal, and sleep came quickly.

In the morning, the ritual of washing up with cold water poured from the pitcher into the bowl was carried out as fast as possible. The sudsy water was emptied from the bowl into a pail hidden behind the doors on the lower part of the commode. Soon I was dressed and downstairs to the warm kitchen for a breakfast of fruit, corn flakes or hot oatmeal, eggs, homemade bread, preserves, and milk, and then outside ... for another day in the wondrous "other world" of one little farm.

Breakfast.

Afterword

Aunt Carrie passed away in 1940 at the age of sixty-two while I was away at the university. Unable to work the farm alone, Uncle Frank rented the house to one neighbor, the land to another, and went to live with his brother Mike in Seattle.

In 1949 he remarried, and after living in California for twenty years and Mississippi for seven, he died in 1975 at the age of ninety-one. He and Aunt Carrie are buried in the little cemetery a half-mile up the road from their farm.

In 1961, Uncle Frank had given up the farm, selling the land to the county for incorporation into the new Hawthorne Hills County Park golf course. Five years later, just after the farm buildings had been razed, the newly-formed Ozaukee County Historical Society began a collection of 19th-century buildings. They started with a donated log house which was moved and re-erected on the site of what had been the Brott farmyard.

This became the nucleus for what is now Pioneer Village, a well-known tourist attraction. Its twenty-three buildings are

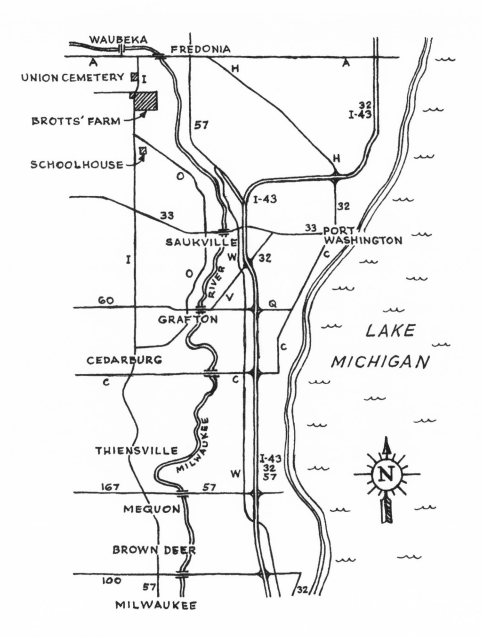

Map of area.

furnished as they would have been in the 1800s, and include residences, shops, outbuildings, a chapel, and a railroad depot. Annual events include sales, socials, contests, exhibitions, festivals, and the popular Handwerkerschau (Handicrafter Show) with dozens of demonstrations.

Pioneer Village is open to the public from noon to five on Wednesdays, Saturdays, and Sundays from Memorial Day weekend to Labor Day, and weekends only through the 2nd Sunday in October. For more information, write Ozaukee County Historical Society, PO Box 206, Cedarburg, WI 53012.

If you visit, you will be walking where Frank and Carrie Brott's farmstead once stood ... and where I explored nearly every inch of the grounds and buildings with such enthusiasm as a boy. The largest portion of the farm, where the crops were grown and the cattle grazed, is now part of the surrounding county park and golf course.

About the Author

Donald S. Henning, born and raised in Milwaukee, began drawing as a child and writing while at the University of Wisconsin-Madison, where he got his B.S. in Mechanical Engineering and minored in Art. After army service he studied industrial design. He also took piano lessons and did portraiture, and through them met and married Carol, with whom he has shared forty-seven years, living for the most part in Ozaukee County, Wisconsin. They now reside in the village of Grafton. While practicing Professional Engineering as a consultant in product design, he side-lined in graphic design and had prose, poetry, and drawings published. For many years Don and Carol were the country's top crewel needlework designers. His hobbies are sketching, painting, and making Early American furniture; hers are gardening and interior decorating. Their Henning Studio creates logos, brochures, and renderings, and Don has designed entrance signage for numerous subdivisions and business parks in southeastern Wisconsin. Their son, Paul, his wife, Mary Ann, and a new grandson, Graham, live in Milwaukee.